SOMERSET
THEN & NOW
IN COLOUR

NICK CHIPCHASE

The History Press

First published in 2012

The History Press
The Mill, Brimscombe Port
Stroud, Gloucestershire, GL5 2QG
www.thehistorypress.co.uk

ISBN 978 0 7524 7004 7

Typesetting and origination by The History Press
Manufacturing managed by Jellyfish Print Solutions Ltd
Printed in India.

CONTENTS

ACKNOWLEDGEMENTS

All of the early photographs were taken by Henry Montague Cooper, and all of the modern photographs by the author, who would like to thank the churchwarden of Norton Fitzwarren church for permission to take photos from the top of the tower and Vicky Breeze for typing and help with the text.

ABOUT THE AUTHOR

Nick Chipchase was born in Trull and now lives in nearby Taunton. Now retired from the insurance business, he is interested in social history, photography and shipwreck research. He has a personal collection of 6,000 local history photographs and postcards.

Henry Montague Cooper's business letterhead

INTRODUCTION

All of the old photographs in this book were taken by local photographer Henry Montague Cooper around 1904 to 1906. Unlike national photographers, Henry took scenes of villages and the countryside during his travels around Somerset in one of the county's first motor cars. His photographic record of Somerset surpasses that of every other local photographer.

Heraclitus (500 BC) referred to change as the only constant and this is true. Somerset reflects many changes seen elsewhere in Britain but some are more muted. In the 1900s Somerset had a population of 434,000, which has now increased to 600,000, representing slower population growth than elsewhere in the United Kingdom. In fact, many rural areas of Somerset saw a population decrease between the two world wars, during the agricultural depression. Some villages never recovered and current growth has been restricted by a huge rise in the value of rural properties. Today's trend is back towards urban living and 'affordable housing' like high-density estates and apartment blocks. It seems probable that this will continue.

The rise in rural affluence is now driven by retirees and those with enough money to escape the urban environment. In the post war era, the countryside was full of dilapidated cottages and barns but nearly all of these have now been renovated to high-value residences by people chasing the rural idyll. Somerset's 'Ag Lab' (agricultural labourers) are now an endangered species.

The countryside has changed dramatically, and there has been a move away from arable farming to pasture. Surprisingly, however, there are many more trees in today's landscape than in the past. Even urban development supports this growth, as garden trees replace open fields, which is also true of upland areas like Dulverton and Minehead. However, the mechanisation of farming has resulted in the loss of hedgerows and flail cutting, the loss of trees in hedges bordering roads.

Somerset's traditional industries have gone: few textile factories remain, heavy industry and mining have declined and quarrying has been centralised to bigger extraction sites away from population centres. The construction of the M5 motorway through Somerset has resulted in urban infill and the rise of massive industrial estates. Taunton ceased to be a market town after nearly 1,000 years when the livestock market moved to a big new complex on junction 24, and the area is also starting to see the construction of high rise apartments, unheard of in former years but now appearing due to a relaxation of planning rules.

Somerset continues to change as trends occur and sometimes reverse, and although change is constant it is also unpredictable, particularly as technology progresses. Will Somerset still be such a pleasant, largely rural county in a hundred years time? I certainly hope so.

ASHBRITTLE

THE PHOTOGRAPH BELOW is of Ashbrittle, a village 6 miles west of Wellington. In 1901 the population of the parish was 325. At that time nearly all trade in Ashbrittle was connected to agriculture. James Lamprey also ran a Temperance Hotel in the village in the early twentieth century. This photograph is from around 1906.

THE VILLAGE, RELATIVELY untouched by modern development, still retains a certain amount of old-fashioned charm; indeed, in 2002 the population of Ashbrittle stood at only 213! Telegraph poles, cars and a modern dustbin denote the present day but the cottages have changed little in a hundred years. In more recent times, it was discovered that the village had a connection with the *Titanic*: local resident Richard Parsons was an eighteen-year-old saloon steward who lost his life on the ship's fated maiden voyage. In 2002, Ashbrittle's famous yew tree was included in a list of great British trees compiled by The Tree Council.

BISHOP'S HULL

THE OLD PHOTOGRAPH below shows Church Row, Bishop's Hull, c.1906. Most early views are characterised by stark Edwardian uniformity, and this photograph, with obedient-looking, uniformly-dressed children, is no different. Bishop's Hull is almost a suburb of Taunton now, but the centre retains some of its original charm. The cottages could not be located on the Census

by name, but we do know that Percy Merson lived at No. 1 during the First World War and that he formed a group of lady bellringers for St Peter's church.

TODAY THE OLD cottages have been modernised, and each occupant has stamped their own individuality on their home. Bishop's Hull now forms part of Taunton's urban extension westward, with further new homes being added at the village extremity. This will bring the village population up to around 4,000 – 4 times the figure of 100 years ago. Now only the railway and the River Tone separate Bishop's Hull and Norton Fitzwarren, which together have a population of nearly 7,000 people.

FROG STREET, BISHOP'S LYDEARD

THE ROW OF cottages on the left in the 1905 picture of Frog Street, Bishop's Lydeard (below) were gutted by fire in April 1906 and subsequently demolished. Montague Cooper's 12hp Belgica Y388

motor car is parked in the road. The car was a twin-cylinder model built by a cycle company established in Brussels in 1885. The company exhibited a six-cylinder 58hp model at the 1908 Agricultural Hall Show in London.

FROG STREET WAS the lowest part of Mount Street, and there used to be a stream here before the estates were developed. The fire-ravaged cottages were replaced by two further cottages in 1908 and Mount Street Garage was built here. The garage, in turn, was replaced by Lydeard Mead in 1997.

Bishop's Lydeard today is a popular commuter village for Taunton and has nearly quadrupled in size since 1902. The former village mill, adjacent to a spacious miller's house, is now a rural life museum.

GORE SQUARE, BISHOP'S LYDEARD

THE SQUARE, BISHOP'S Lydeard, in around 1904. The Lethbridge Arms, formerly the Gore Inn, which can be seen in the old photograph (right), takes its name from the Lethbridge family who lived at Sandhill Park from 1767 to 1913. Sandhill Park has an interesting history: it housed German and Austrian prisoners in the First World War and became a military hospital in the Second World War.

In 1901 Joseph Heydin and his wife Mary ran the pub, employing locally-born Florence Gange as a general servant.

The name above the shop doorway reads 'Comer Sadler': the premises belonged to T.R. Comer, a saddler and harness maker. In the pub car park is a well-preserved Fives wall.

TODAY GORE SQUARE no longer sits on the main traffic route as Bishop's Lydeard now has a bypass. The Lethbridge Arms is still a popular inn and looks to be in much better repair than it did a century ago, with its neat, white-painted exterior. In fact, the only thing spoiling the modern-day photograph are the numerous cars cluttering the roadside.

BLAGDON HILL

BLAGDON VILLAGE, *c*.1905
(right). In the centre is the
Mission Room, built in 1878,
and just behind it is the gable
over the entrance to the
Lamb and Flag Inn. Behind
the cottages on the right is
the former White Lion, then
owned by Hanbury and
Cotching. The landlord was
William Warren, who was
also the local wheelwright.

TODAY BLAGDON HILL is
a popular place to live with
retirees and people working
in Taunton. Now much
more upmarket than in its
rural past, it boasts its own
Indian restaurant, formerly

the White Lion Inn. The little chapel still remains but is now used as a showroom by a bespoke kitchen furniture company. The early view looks remarkably sparse compared to the 2011 photograph above, and many more trees now inhabit the landscape. The Blackdown Hills in the distance were heavily planted with conifer in the past but much of this is currently being felled with the intention of returning the hills to their more natural state.

ST MARY'S CHURCH AND CORNHILL, BRIDGWATER

ST MARY'S CHURCH and Cornhill, Bridgwater, in around 1905 (below). This area is the heart of the market town of Bridgwater, and the 175ft spire of St Mary's has dominated the town's skyline since 1367. The market building and the landmark dome were built in 1823 by Mr Thomas Hutchings

of Bridgwater. Public subscriptions raised over £1,200 for the casting of the bronze statue of Admiral Blake, which was unveiled on the Cornhill in 1900 by Lord Brassey.

CORNHILL IS NOW pedestrianised and the statue of Robert Blake has been moved to a more central position. Some say he is pointing to his birthplace, which is now the site of the Blake Museum, founded in 1926. Unfortunately, he now has to suffer the indignity of having seagulls perching upon his head.

Bridgwater has undergone many changes since the old photograph was taken in 1905. Links to road, rail and sea led to it becoming a major industrial centre, though in many ways traditional industries have declined since then. 2011 saw the completion of the huge Morrisons distribution depot adjacent to the motorway, and south of the town large estates have been built close to the market centre at junction 24.

THE QUAY, BRIDGWATER

THE WONDERFUL OLD photograph below shows the Quay, Bridgwater, *c.* 1906. The town's name most likely comes from the Old Norse *bryggia*, meaning quay or jetty. This photograph shows the West Quay, the construction of which dates to before 1730. It is thought that there were

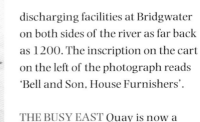

discharging facilities at Bridgwater on both sides of the river as far back as 1200. The inscription on the cart on the left of the photograph reads 'Bell and Son, House Furnishers'.

THE BUSY EAST Quay is now a roadway. Many buildings remain on the West Quay and Starkey, Knight and Ford's flying horse, can be seen on one of them, though the brewery no longer remains. Bridgwater Port Authority still handled 90,000 tons of cargo in 2006, though most of this was stone products, sand and gravel being loaded at Dunball Wharf built in 1844. Little commercial traffic now goes beyond Dunball, and it is likely that the wharf will see increased trade during further construction at the Hinkley Point power station.

BREAN DOWN

ROCKS AT BREAN Down, *c.*1905 (right). At this time the coast from Burnham to Brean Down was completely undeveloped. It was a quiet spot even after the Second World War and it was still possible to walk on the beach in relative solitude. Now the area is jam-packed with holiday resorts and caravan parks. The mile-long walk along Brean Down takes you to the old fortification at the end, which was completed in 1870. In 1900 a huge explosion occurred at the fort when a soldier fired his gun into one of the magazines.

BREAN AND BERROW are now the focus of a huge expansion in holiday camps and caravan sites. The sands are popular and the quiet days of the 1950s have gone, though the very end of the beach near Brean Down is still relatively quiet. The old cottage has been replaced by chalets and a bird garden, behind which a footpath leaves the beach and takes walkers to the old fort at the end of the Down.

Land sailing has been developing here since the 1920s; early yachts were made from the remains of First World War aircraft, though today more sophisticated machines can reach 60mph.

THE REGATTA SPORTS, BURNHAM

EARLY REGATTAS WERE focussed on sporting events which took place on the beach. They nearly always attracted large crowds, as can be seen in this lively scene, photographed in around 1905 (right), which shows Burnham Esplanade. The bandstand which can be seen in the distance was built on an iron pier.

THE ESPLANADE IS still home to several early nineteenth-century properties.

The pavilion (centre) was built on a concrete pier between 1911 and 1914. It fell into disrepair but was restored in 1968. Today's sea wall and defences appear rather bleak compared to the 1905 scene, but they are necessary and successfully prevented destruction in a violent storm in 1981. In future decades, even these defences may have to be extended. The regatta still takes place, although now on a much smaller scale than in its heyday in the early 1900s.

CHARD

THE VIEW OF the High Street below shows a United Patriots Procession in Chard, *c.*1907. Behind the procession, the spire of the Congregational church in Fore Street can be seen. It was erected in 1868 but became unsafe and was demolished in 1979 to be replaced with shops. Buckland's shop (left) later became Thorne's Drapers and then the Conservative Club.

ONE COULD SAY that the modern photograph opposite depicts the demise of the chimney pot; at Harvey's Charity, which is just out of view, all sixteen chimneys were replaced in 2007. Chard is

Somerset's highest town and today has a population of around 12,000, making it a fairly quiet place, with few of the problems besetting larger towns. Two major Victorian transport routes, the canal and railway, are now closed. The last commercial goods rail traffic ran in 1966. A replica model of an aeroplane stands in the main street. It was erected to celebrate the invention of John Stringfellow supposedly resulting in the world's first powered flight in 1848.

COMBE FLOREY

COMBE FLOREY VILLAGE, *c*.1906 (above). In the distance is the school – now a private house.
The school was built in about 1848 and subsequently enlarged to accommodate seventy children.

At that time it was run by Thomas Lilley and his wife. In 1902 the population of Combe Florey was 260, at which time it had no post office or public house, though there were two blacksmiths and a small village shop.

COMBE FLOREY SCHOOL closed in the 1950s, and the village's population has declined over the years from 260 in 1902 to 252 in 2002. The school building, which had consisted of one big room with tall windows, is still standing, and its current owners have created a lovely garden. Although not in the village, the local pub The Farmer's Arms, situated on the main road to Minehead, remains a popular venue and was nominated the winner of the best kept cellars award in 2010. Combe Florey House is the largest property in the village and was at one time the home of the novelist Evelyn Waugh and later of his son Auberon, both of whom are buried in the village.

CORFE

CORFE, A VILLAGE 4 miles south of Taunton, can be seen looking south in this photograph of around 1904. In 1901 Corfe had its own post office, church, chapel and school and a population of 383. The chapel, visible on the left of the old photograph, was built in 1897 and is now a

private house. Corfe's church is dedicated to St Nicholas and is Norman in style, having been rebuilt around the middle of the nineteenth century when the south aisle was added and the church tower rebuilt. In 1969 the chancel was further restored.

THE WHITE HART Inn, on the right of the old postcard, is now obscured by trees. Chapel Cottage was sold for £227,500 in 2006, an indication of just how popular this type of converted property has become. The population of Corfe has declined over the years, and was only 262 in 2002. As a result, Corfe remains largely unspoilt by urban development.

CORFE VICARAGE AND SCHOOL

IN THIS 1904 view (right), looking north, the vicarage is on the right. Peter Brancker was the vicar and he lived here with his wife Florence and three servants. In 1898 the vicar had electric lighting installed in the church at a cost of just over £53 (roughly £4,500 in today's money). Montague Cooper's MMC car stands in the road.

The school accommodated ninety children from Corfe and Orchard Portman and had electricity installed in 1904. The building is now a private house and a war memorial,

which commemorates the residents of Corfe who fell in the First and Second World War, stands where the elm tree is. Twelve residents of Corfe from the First World War appear on the memorial and just two from the second, both of whom were members of the Volunteer Reserve.

THE EARLY VIEW reminds us how large and palatial vicarages used to be. The hedge and wall remain today but now the trees completely obscure the building. Even so, the modern photograph on the left displays a much more formal view with a well delineated road and tidy verges. The old elm tree has long gone together with millions of others in the landscape when Dutch elm disease ravaged the countryside. The disease reached the UK in 1927 but a more virulent strain introduced in the late 1960s killed off most of the trees as they began to reach maturity.

CREECH ST MICHAEL

THIS PHOTOGRAPH ILLUSTRATES quite clearly Mr Cooper's method of work: he has arrived by car and attracted a group of inquisitive children, who happily posed for his photograph. This view shows North End with Laurel Villa on the left. Just out of view to the right is Northend Mill, owned at the time the photograph was taken by Joseph Loader. The water that powered the mill came from the River Tone, known locally as 'the Preen', which runs through Northend.

LIKE MANY SOMERSET villages, Creech St Michael has seen large changes in population. In 1801 the village had 628 souls and the population had increased to 1,700 by 1841. At the time of the previous photograph, from around 1905, the village population was 1,166. Levels dropped below 1,000 between 1911 and 1951, but the introduction of main sewerage in the 1950s paved the way for rapid development in the 1960s, when many new houses were built. Today, around 2,500 people live in Creech St Michael, which has become a popular commuter village for Taunton workers. However, it must be admitted that today the village has lost a little of its original charm due to the introduction of traffic calming, a roundabout and tall street lamps.

CROWCOMBE

CROWCOMBE VILLAGE AND cross, *c.*1906 (below). In the distance is the Carew Arms Inn, originally the Lion or Three Lions but renamed in 1814. Crowcombe once had a market and fair, and a fourteenth-century cross marks the site on a triangle of grass. Like many villages in the area, the population has declined. In 1831 it stood at 691 but had dropped to 405 by 1951.

Crowcombe Village.

In 2002 population levels had risen again to 590. Crowcombe had a manor house as early as 1295 and the present Crowcombe Court was started in about 1723.

AS USUAL, TREES dominate the present landscape, and the Carew Arms is now obscured in this modern view. The delightful thatched cottage and orchard are gone, but the cross and grass area remain. The Crowcombe Court Estate was created in 1894 and it is said that the construction of the Court itself involved the felling of 500 local oak trees in 1725. Agricultural use around the village has progressed from arable to grassland, with 84 per cent of farmland under grass by 1976.

CHURCHINFORD

THE YORK INN, Churchinford, *c.*1905 (below). In some parts the building dates to the sixteenth century, and it still retains an open fireplace and oak beams. Walter Doble held the licence at the time of the photograph. He was a local man and ran the inn with his wife, Jane, and a teenage servant.

CHURCHINFORD STILL RETAINS its village pub although, like most other village properties, the thatched roof has gone. The village has a picturesque setting within the Blackdown Hills Area of Outstanding Natural Beauty. Rural public houses are, in effect, fighting a rear guard action to preserve their declining numbers; 2009 saw an interesting statistic emerge when, for the first time, there were more supermarkets in the UK than public houses. Five thousand public houses have gone in the last decade alone, reducing current numbers to below 55,000. It is a trend likely to continue as smaller villages lose amenities no longer necessary with the increase in people using personal instead of public transport and using the Internet for shopping and other services. When this photograph was taken in 2011, a select development of houses were being constructed in the village.

DUNKERY
AND
WHEDDON
CROSS

THIS EARLY PHOTOGRAPH (right) from around 1906 gives a view of the southern slope of Dunkery Hill above Bin Combe and Mansley Combe. The road from Wheddon Cross passes the head of Mansley Combe through Dunkery Gate and then skirts the highest point in Somerset, the 1,705ft Dunkery Beacon, to drop down again to Luccombe.

STILL A BEAUTIFUL spot, the beacon is at the very centre of the Exmoor National Park and is a representative of a preserved and well-managed

landscape. It was given to the National Trust by Sir Thomas Acland and others along with the rest of Holnicote Estate. Sadly the beacon can no longer be called the highest point in Somerset as it has been eclipsed by the Mendip transmitter mast at 586 metres. Wheddon Cross now forms part of Cutcombe. Jointly, the villages retain many of their original amenities including a school, post office and public house. The area is at the heart of the Exmoor farming community, hosting one of the only livestock markets within the National Park.

DULVERTON

THE TOWN OF Dulverton can trace its history back to Saxon times and is mentioned in the Domesday Book of 1086. Dulverton is the southern gateway to Exmoor and retains much of its old-world charm. The town's 1,300-strong population remains very much the same as it did 100 years ago. This wonderful bird's-eye view of Dulverton dates from around 1906 and has been taken from Cottage Lane above the River Barle.

THE MODERN PHOTOGRAPH above, taken from the cottage garden, the only vantage point now available, typifies the changes in rural landscape over the last 100 years. Contrary to expectation, trees are far more numerous now and many early twentieth-century views are difficult to replicate.

Dulverton is now a popular tourist centre and forms a gateway to the Exmoor National Park, and the park authority has its headquarters here. The town railway station closed in the 1960s. It had served as a junction station for the Exe Valley Railway. The town was affected by the same flooding that devastated Lynton and Lynmouth in 1952.

DUNSTER

DUNSTER VILLAGE AND yarn market can be seen in the old photograph below, *c*.1906. A classic Somerset view, this part of Dunster has been photographed by many postcard publishers. The yarn market was built in 1609 as Dunster was an important cloth-making centre, and market day was the biggest event for miles around. Dunster has a beach about half a mile south of the village centre and a station on the West Somerset Railway.

IN ESSENCE LITTLE has changed at Dunster, and what change has taken place can only be seen in the detail of the two views. Fashion and transport have evolved and the modern photograph above shows the diminished spaciousness we see so often. Dunster has 200 Grade II listed buildings and little material change can be expected in the future. The Luttrell Arms on the left remains, as does Dunster Castle, which was given to the National Trust in 1976 and has recently been refurbished. Much of the present structure dates to remodelling in Victorian times, with the addition of towers and turrets giving the present-day castle a fairytale appearance. Dunster by Candlelight – a recent tradition – takes place at the castle early in December every year.

EXFORD

THE CROWN HOTEL, Exford, *c*.1906 (right). Ethel Amery, a widow, ran the hotel in 1901, but by the time of the old photograph the name of J.H. Tarr appears on the building. The Exmoor Stores, with their delivery van outside, was owned by Walter E. Batchelor, a native of Rotherhithe. He lived with his wife Annie and young son Leslie. They were sufficiently well-off to be able to afford a servant and domestic nurse. Again, the car probably belonged to Mr Cooper.

BOTH THE CROWN Hotel and Exmoor Stores remain today.

The village has a well manicured appearance and the tiny village green remains, though local parents raised money for the fine children's playground opposite The Stores in 1999. The village remains a popular destination for horse riders and walkers. The Crown Inn caters for both and offers three acres of gardens as well as a stable yard. The village lies at the very centre of the Exmoor National Park.

EAST BRENT

THE CROSSWAYS, EAST Brent, *c*.1906 (right). This view shows Alfred Emery's Brent Knoll Inn. He ran this hostelry with his wife Elizabeth, assisted by her father, brother and sister. The war memorial was erected opposite the inn on the junction of the A370 and the Old Bristol Road in 1921. The stonemason was Mr Emery of Burnham-on-Sea and the memorial commemorates sixteen parishoners and their relatives who fell in the First World War as well as two souls lost from The Second World War and Korean War.

THE CROSSWAYS HAVE been relegated to a backwater in recent times as the main route no longer passes by the Brent Knoll Inn. The pub is very traditional and was called 'one of Somerset's little gems' in a recent online review from a customer. Visitors are attracted by a nearby garden centre, popular with coach parties. Brent Knoll itself, so clearly visible from the M5 motorway, offers splendid views of the surrounding countryside.

HUNTSPILL

HUNTSPILL AND ILEX Stores, *c.*1905 (right). Mr Cooper produced this card for Gilbert Burnett, the owner of Ilex Stores. On the back is written 'Hope to call upon you on or about Mon 5th Sept. when your commands will be esteemed and receive prompt attention.' Gilbert Burnett was born in Huntspill in about 1870 and lived with his wife Annie. The couple employed one servant. The 1901 Census describes Gilbert as a draper, grocer and general shopkeeper and his store, dating from 1792, took its name from an Ilex tree in the garden. The premises are now Ilex Court.

THE MODERN PHOTOGRAPH on the left exhibits much in the way of recent change. Gone are the subtleties, softness and irregularity of the old view. Today's view has angularity and neatness. The old stores frontage can still be seen but the meandering pavement edge and low hedges are gone. There is a starkness in the modern view. Today we have the need to reduce everything to a level of minimal management. January 2007 saw the 400th anniversary of the Great Bristol Channel Flood, reminding us that natural events can still change the environment we occupy. The floods affected an area of 200 square miles including Huntspill. An estimated 3,000 people were killed.

HALSE

THE SCHOOL, HALSE, *c*.1905 (right). The building dates from 1856, and thirty-five children attended the school in 1905. Indeed, most of them seem to have followed Mr Cooper around during his visit. The school was given to the education authority in 1939 when the estate was sold by the young lord of the manor, Hugh Graham Evelyn Dunsterville.

IT IS IMPOSSIBLE to recreate the old photograph today as the tree on the little green where the children sat has grown to tall proportions. The school has undergone a few alterations and is now a private house.

Unusually, the cottage next door still retains a thatched roof. Today Halse has an air of quiet respectability akin to the 'midsomer' villages of television fiction. In modern parlance one would call the village 'unspoilt' though that implies that no change has taken place. The village population is less now than it was one hundred years ago, and its appearance suggests that it is an affluent retirement village rather than popular with commuting workers; certainly, levels of property occupancy are less. The village pub is called The New Inn but dates to the eighteenth century and was formerly a coaching inn.

HATCH STATION

HATCH STATION CAN be seen in the old photograph in about 1905. The station is a Grade II listed building and now a small industrial site. The station is situated just south of the 152-yard Hatch tunnel on the Taunton to Chard branch. It was built between 1864 and 1866. The main building is of brick with ashlar dressing with a Welsh slate roof. The station had a single platform on the down

side and a goods loop on the up side. The signal-box was built on the up side of the goods loop. The 1 34-mile branch line opened in 1866. In 1956 the goods loop and signal-box closed, and as a result of the Beeching Report, passenger traffic ceased on the whole branch in 1962.

HATCH BEAUCHAMP HAS developed rather differently from most Somerset villages. The village is remarkably industrial and most of this industry centres around the old chalet-style station building. The village had a population of 386 in 1902 and this now stands at around 575. It no longer sits on the main traffic route as the village has a bypass. John Rouse Merriott Chard, VCRE, is buried here. The hero of Rorke's Drift died of cancer of the tongue in 1897.

HIGHBRIDGE
GWR STATION

HIGHBRIDGE GWR STATION,
c.1906. The station was opened
in 1841 by the Bristol & Exeter
Railway on what is now the
Great Western Main Line (the
Great Western Railway took
control of the station in 1876).
An adjoining station was added
by the Somerset Central Railway
in 1854. This later became the
Somerset & Dorset Joint Railway.
The GWR station became
Highbridge and Burnham-on-Sea
station in 1962.

THE MODERN PHOTOGRAPH
shows the station from the

road bridge. The adjacent Somerset and Dorset station has been developed as a modern housing estate. A pair of wagon wheels on a short section of line remind one of Highbridge's important railway past. Today the station serves as an unmanned stop for Highbridge and Burnham, being renamed as such in 1991. The original buildings have been demolished and the footbridge shortened following the closure of the S. and D. Platforms in early 1970s. The station is now an

G. W. R. Station.

eerily quiet modern station, in essence symbolising the reduction of manual labour in favour of the automation of services – the latter an accelerating trend in today's society.

HIGHBRIDGE

HIGHBRIDGE FROM THE GWR station, *c*.1906 (below). At this time the town was also an important industrial centre but this has since declined. In 1933 Highbridge was sublimated within the joint town council district of Highbridge and Burnham-on-Sea. Before this the town's population was 2,585. This view shows the Cooper's Arms Hotel run in 1901 by Mrs Alice Card, a widow, and her son Robert.

AS WE SEE so often, modern day foliage masks much of the older view. The Cooper's Arms can still be seen but has not been so successful in recent years having had a succession of tenants after the freehold was sold. In truth, Highbridge has declined from its industrial days when the Somerset and Dorset wagon works employed 400 people. The railway has lost much of its commercial freight and the town wharf closed in 1949. The sublimation with Burnham-on-Sea is still not popular with some residents, though a referendum held in 2001 was unsuccessful. Highbridge still has a sense of its former past, and a local community group published a study of the town's history to celebrate the station's 150th anniversary in 2004.

KINGSTON ST MARY

KINGSTON ST MARY village, *c*.1904. The thatched cottages in the background were demolished in about 1920. The gabled building housed Amphlett's Kingston Stores in 1909. The car Y308 is Montague Cooper's 9hp MMC, which he acquired in 1904. The Motor Manufacturing Company was established by H.J. Lawson, initially in Coventry. Production ceased in about 1908 after the company had moved to Clapham. A 12hp Belgica replaced the MMC after a short while. Note

the photographer has captured this scene in good, bright light, probably in the summer; the muddy roads of winter are seldom seen in postcards from the 1900s.

IN THE 2011 picture, today's photographer's car stands in the same position as his predecessor's, and the building formerly marked as 'Post Office' is now partially obscured by bushes. John McAdam (1756-1836) initiated the changes seen in today's roads; broken stones and dust gave way to water-bound McAdam. After 1900 the advent of faster motor cars resulted in much dust arising from the low pressure caused by the passing vehicle. Tar-bound McAdam solved this problem and in turn this was replaced by modern mixed asphalt (black top) in the 1920s.

KINGSTON ST MARY
CONTINUED

THE BIRD'S-EYE view of Kingston St Mary, a parish and village 3 miles north of Taunton, below dates from around 1905. Kingston St Mary lies under the southern extremity of the Quantock Hills. The parish once belonged to the kings of the West Saxons, hence its name 'The Kings Settlement'. Only in the 1950s was the name of the village church, St Mary's, added to the

village name. The splendid west tower of the church was built in 1490.

BOTH VIEWS SHOW the village and Taunton Deane away to the west. The modern view is taken from the village reservoir being slightly north of the earlier viewpoint. Only the church tower can now be seen and much of the village appears to be covered by trees. In essence little has changed here and even today's population remains as it was 100 years ago. What has changed within this view relates to social conditions: gone are the dilapidated labourer's cottages, almost all of which have been bought and refurbished by affluent owners. This is a common modern solution for those desiring a home in the countryside, where planning controls may limit the building of new properties.

KILVE

KILVE VILLAGE, *c.*1906 (right).
Kilve lies on the A39 midway
between Bridgwater and Minehead.
This view shows the Hood Arms
Hotel, a seventeenth-century
coaching inn. The brewery firm of
Starkey, Knight and Ford owned the
premises at this time. The landlord
was the appropriately named
Amos Wine, formerly a carpenter
from Bicknoller. The lane next to
the inn leads down to Kilve beach,
where the remains of an oil-shale
extraction plant can be seen. This
was installed in the 1920s but the
business soon became defunct.

TODAY THE HOOD Arms is the
epitome of neatness and modernity

but still retains a charming, old-fashioned interior. The garden and wall have been sacrificed
to accommodate the passing motor car but outwardly much is the same. Only those modern
contrivances, the ubiquitous telegraph pole and road markings, in some way mar the scene. The
original inn at Kilve was called the Chough and Anchor but by 1832 it was named as the Hood
Arms. Today the inn caters for visitors wishing to explore the natural beauty of the Quantock Hills
and the dramatic coastal scenery, which is now an Area of Outstanding Natural Beauty, the first to
be established in the UK in 1957.

MINEHEAD AND
NORTH HILL

MINEHEAD, THE BAY and North Hill, *c*.1904 (below). In 1087 the Manor of Minehead had a
population of sixty-nine. Like several seaside towns in Somerset it developed into a popular resort
during the nineteenth century and by 1901 had a population of 2,511. Numerous fine hotels
were built and a pier was added in 1901 by the Campbell Steamboat Company. The pier was 700ft

long but unfortunately it was removed during the Second World War as it was in the way of a gun emplacement.

ANOTHER SET OF views that typify the evolution from open fields to wooded slopes, James Date's view of North Hill (from around 1875) shows a landscape almost devoid of trees, where the field pattern reflects that of medieval times. Minehead made the progression from a mid-Victorian rural economy to an Edwardian seaside resort and then experienced a revival in popularity, which was encouraged by the re-opening of the railway and Butlins holiday camp. In the distance is Quay Street leading to the harbour. Here stood Lamb Cottage, demolished around 1911. A great storm affected houses on the seaward side of Quay Street in the same year, and they were also removed.

MINEHEAD, MARKET HOUSE AND SQUARE

MARKET HOUSE AND Square, Minehead, *c.*1904 (right). This new building was erected in 1902 to replace the smaller one, then known as the Fish Market. Note the sapling trees on the right-hand side of the photograph.

THE OLD PLUME of Feathers Hotel in the middle distance has been replaced by a modern block, which is somehow at odds with its ornate surroundings. James Date, a local photographer, shows a similar view from around 1875 in his book *James*

Date's Exmoor and West Somerset, with newly planted trees that are possibly those that we see today and which now obscure much of the fine architecture. The Market House clock still just manages to peep through the now large trees. Much of Minehead's Edwardian architecture remains, and it was the architect W.J. Tamlyn who was responsible for many of the fine buildings, which are constructed from local sandstone and red Bridgwater tiles, still evident in the modern photograph.

MINEHEAD VIEWED
FROM NORTH HILL

BIRD'S-EYE VIEW towards Dunster, *c.*1904. During the sixteenth century all the flat land was sea.
It came up to Conygar Hill and Dunster had a harbour. Much of the seaward side is now the Butlins
holiday camp. Smoke can be seen rising from Minehead station. The railway came in 1874, and

British Railways closed the line in 1971; the whole line back to Bishop's Lydeard is now run by the West Somerset Railway.

NOWADAYS IT IS almost impossible to recreate the view of around 1905. We peep between tall fir trees for today's view above, though perhaps we could see more from one of the windows of the large houses below Beacon Road. We can see, however, the remarkable growth that has taken place in Minehead.

Much of the beach was washed away during a severe storm in 1990. As a result, 1.8km of new sea wall was built and 320,000 tons of sand imported to replace the beach. The new sea defences were officially opened in 2001. The West Somerset Railway, which terminates at Minehead, is the longest heritage railway in Britain. The South West Coast Path National Trail starts at a marker erected at the town in 2001. It travels the South West Peninsular Coast to Poole in Dorset.

NETHER STOWEY

ST MARY'S CHURCH and clock tower, Nether Stowey, *c.*1906 (right). Nether Stowey is a busy village just off the A39 between Minehead and Bridgwater. Its bypass was constructed in 1968 and the older part of the village is a conservation area. The village is famous for its links with two Romantic poets; Samuel Taylor Coleridge lived in the village between 1797 and 1799 at the same time as William Wordsworth and his sister Dorothy lived at nearby Alfoxton House, and the two poets became close friends. The clock tower in this photograph was built for Queen Victoria's Diamond Jubilee in 1897.

NETHER STOWEY TODAY has the air of a small town but Coleridge and Wordsworth would still no doubt recognise the village as only details have changed. The George Inn now has a bright tile façade and the village still has two other pubs. There has been some growth in housing, possibly due in part to the nearby Hinkley Point power station. The village is rich in history and is still overlooked by the Norman motte and bailey castle. Local resident John Walford is remembered by the nearby Walford's Gibbet, the place his body was hung for the murder of his wife in 1789.

NORTH CURRY

NORTH CURRY, *c.*1905 (right). On the extreme left is London House, where Thomas Giblett had a shop which appears in directories from 1889 to 1923. He produced his own postcards of North Curry. The gas lamp was replaced by a war memorial in 1920. The old brewery is the building to the right, which is a Grade II listed building originating from the late seventeenth century. James Temlett was the occupier at this time.

A PROFUSION OF trees now mask the old brewery and Giblett's little shop is long gone. Although having grown much in the last 100 years, North Curry supports only a few more people than it did a century ago. Such is the change in occupancy levels from the days when many villages contained agricultural workers and their large families. A massive upsurge in rural affluence has changed Somerset's villages more than any other factor. The war memorial still stands, now adjacent to the inevitable signpost, whilst the little chain fence looks to be original. As ever, the shiny new cars are at odds with the soft pastel colours of the local buildings.

NORTON FITZWARREN – VIEW SOUTH

WHERE POSSIBLE, MR Cooper would climb to the top of the village church tower for his 'bird's eye views' like this one of Norton below. The buildings of the Taunton Cider Factory have yet to be built.

Norton station (far right), the footbridge and the Railway Hotel can all be seen in this photograph from around 1904.

IN RECENT YEARS all the buildings of the Taunton Cider Factory were demolished, and new housing is growing at a fast pace as Norton Fitzwarren finds itself in the middle of a population boom; the village grew from 642 people in 1901 to 2,325 in 2002! No doubt the 3,000 mark will soon be passed. The village outskirts are now home to the new Somerset Heritage Centre and the headquarters of Royal Military 40 Commando. The West Somerset Railway now owns land to the west of the village. The modern view above shows the hotel, now a burnt out ruin, in the centre of a clump of trees. The Railway Hotel played a part in the treatment of injured passengers in the famous 1940 railway crash.

PITMINSTER

PITMINSTER POST OFFICE and school, *c*.1905 (right). Miss Joan Upham was postmistress in 1910. Although born in Pitminster in about 1852, the 1901 Census places her in Paddington, employed as a lady's maid. The post office (the thatched building) was damaged by a fire in 1955 and a new house was built for Mr and Mrs Lee, the occupants. The school (centre) was built in the parish orchard in 1840 and catered for 101 children when it opened. With numbers declining, the school closed in 1921, reopening briefly during the Second World War for evacuee children from Plaistow.

PITMINSTER IS STILL a large parish with a relatively low population density. The village of the same name is actually smaller than Blagdon Hill, also in the parish. Modern bungalows stand on the site of the old thatched post office adjacent to the former school building, which

is now used for parish activities. Our present-day camera cannot match the wide field of view obtained by Mr Cooper's landscape camera, so we lose that sense of spaciousness seen in the older photograph.

STOGUMBER

A BIRD'S-EYE view of Stogumber,
c.1906 (right). Mr Cooper produced
this card for Frederick Inkpen, a
grocer and draper in Stogumber.
The village lies in a valley between
the Quantocks and the Brendons
at a stream crossing. It was once
described as a small market town
and a brewery was established here
in about 1840. This was begun by
G. Elers, but became Sloman and
Brander in about 1880. The final
owner was Mathew Mossman, who
was at the brewery from about 1904
until 1910. The water from the
brewery came from a spring known
as Harry Hill's Well.

IF STOGUMBER HAD aspirations
to grow into a small town, they

disappeared years ago. Now the village is a tranquil place of pastel cottages and quiet roads, the silence only punctuated on occasion by the whistle of a steam train arriving at the station. The modern view suggests a place of picturesque insularity, tucked away in the trees between the Quantock and Brendon Hills. In the centre of the view is a small sign denoting the village pub The White Horse Inn, a Grade II listed building. The Monksilver road threads its way up the lower slopes of the Brendon Hills. Those fields seen on the right of the old photograph are now larger as hedges have been removed, and the odd scattering of trees, perhaps elms, have given way to more general cover.

STOGURSEY

STOGURSEY VILLAGE, *c.*1905 (below). Mr Cooper has attracted his usual crowd of children in Stogursey's wide main street. The village lies 3 miles from the A39 and the village of Nether Stowey. It is only a mile away from the sea. The village was given to William de Falaise by William

the Conqueror and is recorded as Stoche in the Domesday Book. The village became Stoke Curci or Courcy and is now Stogursey. At the end of the street the Church of St Andrew can be seen; it was built in the early twelfth century by English, rather than Norman, builders.

SOME OF THE wall where the children stood in the old photograph remains, but little else has changed in this neat little village with its twelfth-century church. Some of the church's Victorian extravagance was removed in later years. To the south of the village lies Stogursey Castle of a similar age to the church but badly damaged shortly after construction. The property is now in the care of the Landmark Trust. A red pillar box marks the post office and the all intrusive telegraph poles straddle the view.

TRULL

TRULL VILLAGE, PICTURED here in around 1905, is a parish and village 2 miles south of Taunton. The church is dedicated to All Saints, and in the late nineteenth century the tower was rendered in plaster. The village still retains its primary school, which I attended. The population in 1901

was 960, but this has now increased to over 2,000 due, in part, to the village's proximity to Taunton.

MY FORMER FAMILY home of sixty years lies at the bottom of the hill. The iron railings were removed during the Second World War and have now been replaced by a wooden fence. The church wall has partially been replaced by railings, perhaps to afford a better view of the war memorial. The village still retains its essential services and the original school is much larger now. The old school gate, through which the author travelled many times, remains. Time moves on leaving half forgotten memories, like running a hand down the church wall top until I could no longer touch it. Those were the days when you never left your door locked, the dog slept in the middle of the road and Sunday school was unavoidable each week.

ROCKWELL GREEN

IN THE DISTANCE in the photograph is All Saints' church, which was built in 1889 on land given by Samuel Dobree, and local industrialist Frederick Thomas Elworthy provided financial support. The original church had no spire but one was added in 1907 – quite rare for Somerset. The peal of six bells was installed in 1909. The brick water tower can also be seen here. Water came from springs near Westford and was pumped to the tower from a pumping station powered by gas engines.

A larger concrete tower was built next to the brick tower in 1935.

THE STRONG LIGHT accentuates the detail in this modern view. The church now has its belated spire and the concrete water tower. Far to the right is the Barley Mow public house, which is looking far more resplendent than it did 100 years ago. In truth, one rarely sees a rundown pub property today – perhaps visual appeal is now part of the marketing strategy. Although very close to Wellington, Rockwell Green developed independently and has seen rapid growth in recent years. The village population stood at 1,618 in 1991 but this figure is now close to 2,600 and both Rockwell Green and Wellington effectively conjoined having a combined population of 16,300.

85

TAUNTON TOWN CENTRE

MARKET HOUSE AND Taunton centre, *c.*1904, can be seen in the photograph on the right. This is a less common viewpoint of the town centre, which has been photographed by many postcard publishers. The Market House was built in 1770 but its arcades on the side were removed in 1930. The Kinglake Memorial (centre) was erected in 1867 and demolished in 1934. At this time a market was held on the Parade on Wednesdays and Saturdays but it moved to a new site off Priory Bridge Road in 1929. Taunton has now lost its market town status as a new market site has been built near Bridgwater.

TAUNTON IS THE historic county town of Somerset. Our modern view is animated and un-posed and on closer inspection of the early view we see how everyone is aware of the camera. It has been posed to accommodate the early camera's slow shutter speed. In such a way, technology affects our perception of earlier days. Life then had to wait awhile whilst the photographer completed his work. The accommodation of traffic has changed our towns and villages more than any other factor. Taunton does, however, now have pedestrian areas and more are planned for the future. The town has grown rapidly in the passing century: population has rocketed from 21,000 to over 60,000. Many local people fear increasing development, with some housing targets approaching 18,000.

EAST STREET, TAUNTON

THE LONDON HOTEL, *c.*1904 (right). The occasion is a rally organised by the De Dion Bouton Motor Company in July 1904. The man on the tricycle is Tom Crump, surveyor to the Rural District Council. Ernest H. Claridge took over the hotel in 1901 when he was thirty-one years old. He was assisted by his wife Susan and they employed a barmaid, two hotel book keepers, a kitchen maid, a housemaid, a chambermaid, a cook, an under chambermaid, a pantry maid, a page boy, a boot cleaner and billiard maker. Walter Whittingham, a local wine and spirit merchant, bought the hotel in 1913 and continued to use the same postcard (now altered) for advertising. Whittingham had acquired Scarlett & Sons wine and spirit merchants business in nearby Cheapside at

about the same time. After his death in 1919, his widow sold the hotel to Trust Houses Ltd who renamed it the County Hotel.

THE COUNTY HOTEL has now gone and the building houses Marks & Spencer and Waterstone's book shop. The car rally is a vision of things to come and probably led to Taunton's first traffic jam. Worldwide car use has around 5,000 vehicles in 1904 and now stands close to 600 million. Taunton has faired well in coping with this relentless increase. The M5 motorway constructed between 1967 and 1977 relieved those towns and villages situated on the A38. Taunton's 'Third Way' opened in October 2011 and plans for the Northern Inner Distributer Road are well advanced. This will run close to the massive redevelopment at Taunton's former livestock market. Sadly, it means that Taunton is no longer a market town.

FORE STREET, TAUNTON

MARSHALSEA'S GARAGE, FORE Street, *c.*1912 (right). Left to right are a Darracq, Fiat and Hallford. Mr Van Trump is the figure on the right. As well as charabancs, Hallfords also built lorries and buses. Darracq were originally a French company, until taken over by Owen Clegg in about 1913. A merger with Sunbeam Talbot came in 1920. Fiat originally stood for Fabbrica Italiana Automobili Torino (F.I.A.T). Marshalsea Brothers originally started their business at Ilminster and had acquired premises at 55 East Street, Taunton, before January 1911.

GOOD ARCHITECTURE RARELY changes and Taunton still retains a diversity of styles. The ravages of the 1960s redevelopment have not been quite so acute as in other towns. The garage has now gone following a progression of relocation often experienced elsewhere. All too often this has resulted in the wholesale destruction of linear frontages such as seen in Taunton's East Reach, the sale of petrol now requiring large forecourts and pump islands. Taunton is experiencing a period of change by moving away from its old traditional industries and markets. The town museum recently reopened as the refurbished Museum of Somerset. Enhancement of the area in front of the museum is planned. The town has become a pleasant cultural and shopping centre but reservations remain that excessive development in the future could spoil our county town.

WEDMORE

THE GEORGE HOTEL and Church Street, Wedmore, *c.*1905. Thomas Hawkins was the hotel proprietor at this time. He was a local man and lived with his wife Rosina and two step-children. By all accounts the hotel was prosperous as an ostler, domestic servant and a nurse were employed, the latter only twelve years old, in 1901. The band seen here is possibly that of the Salvation Army.

STILL A TRANQUIL scene, with the basic architecture little changed, although the dangerous-looking chimney has gone. The George Hotel presents the same character, though, with an added restaurant called '1760'. The telephone box remains as a symbol of Somerset's pre-digital past. Many have been 'adopted' by the local community although they no longer serve their original function. The Borough at Wedmore is still the heart of commercial life. Today it has the added benefit of a small shopping mall.

WELLS

UNUSUALLY, MR COOPER has given Wrench's postcards a prominent position in this view of
Wells' Market Place from around 1906. The Market Place has been the focal point of the city for
centuries. The shops running towards the cathedral are built on walls created by Thomas Bekynton
in the fifteenth century. He also provided the water supply here in 1451, which still flows.

The Penniless Porch gives access to Cathedral Green.

LARGELY, THE MARKET Place remains untouched by time, and the fine Gothic style cathedral, begun about 1180, still dominates the skyline. The revolutionary new French architectural style has been softened by the lightness of the carving and the use of warm Doulting stone. In recent years much restoration has taken place to the cathedral's impressive west front. Wells has a population of about 10,000 and has had city status since 1205. Following the City of London, it is the smallest city in England. The market cross seen in both photographs is now a Grade II listed building. It was erected in 1797 and replaced Bishop Bekynton's conduit.

95

Other titles published by The History Press

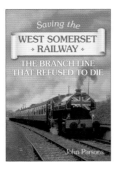

Saving the West Somerset Railway: The Branch Line that Refused to Die

JOHN PARSONS

The West Somerset Railway opened in 1862, linking Taunton, Watchet and Minehead. Popular with tourists travelling the Somerset coast, it was nonetheless closed by British Rail in 1971.This book tells the story of the small group of enthusiasts, many of whom still work on the railway today, who refused to let the line die, a dream that was thwarted not only by British Rail, but also by the rail unions.

978 0 7524 6403 9

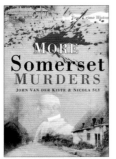

More Somerset Murders

NICOLA SLY & JOHN VAN DER KISTE

This chilling follow-up to *Somerset Murders* brings together more murderous tales that shocked not only the county but made headline news throughout the nation. Covering the length and breadth of Somerset, the featured cases include two female poisoners. A wide variety of means and motives are covered in Nicola Sly and John Van der Kiste's well-illustrated and enthralling text, which will appeal to everyone interested in true-crime history and the shadier side of Somerset's past.

978 0 7524 5742 0

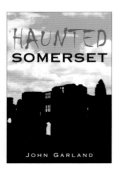

Haunted Somerset

JOHN GARLAND

This collection of stories and twice-told tales from around Somerset lifts the shrouds off many new and legendary hauntings, including some spine-tingling experienes as recounted to the author by Somerset townsfolk, villagers and visitors. Researching historical and contemporary sources. *Haunted Somerset* reveals its uniquely supernatural heritage from a coffin on the road, eerie Bath, the phantoms of Sedgemoor, Dunster Castle's ghostly sightings, headless horsemen, animal apparitions and Exmoor spectres.

978 0 7524 4335 5

Bath: a Pocket Miscellany

TOM BRADSHAW

Did you know that the planet Uranus was discovered from a back garden in Bath? Or that Queen Victoria spurned Bath after its citizens joked about her plump ankles? Bath is a fascinating city with a history stretching back to pre-Roman times. It was the destination of choice for Georgian high society, attracting gamblers, rakes and pleasure-seekers. Today, it is still a popular tourist destination, home to quirky characters, fascinating architecture and an intriguing history.

978 0 7524 6030 7

Visit our website and discover thousands of other History Press books.

www.thehistorypress.co.uk

The History Press